Inspiration Agents Press

Printed in the United States

Is Your Networking Working?

Nurturing Your Network to Abundance

Glen Gould

Benjamin Turpin

Is Your Networking Working?

Table of Contents

Is Your Networking Working?

Nurturing Your Network to Abundance

Forward

Why Is This Book So Important And Needed?

It has been said that people in our society are slowly isolating themselves. With the introduction of personal computers, email, video conferencing and the other conveniences provided by modern technology, we see fewer and fewer real people in our day to day interactions. Often we are conversing and negotiating through a screen.

It is vitally important to engage and interact with people. But where does one learn to do this effectively in our technologically advanced culture? This is one of the many reasons this book is such an important tool to the association or chamber member, business executive or busy mom or dad.

Using the techniques taught in this book you will be able to effectively interact in all networking atmospheres. Whether at the conference or dinner table, business or social mixer; you will become a Power Networker.

You may find it beneficial to visit our website: www.isyournetworkingworking.com and to use the tools we have placed on the site to gauge your networking effectiveness at this time. We encourage you to invest some time using the "Networking Scorecard" and the "Annual Networking Expense Calculator" to assess you current networking skills and effectiveness. Once you have used this book to hone your skills to a new level, revisit the website and take inventory of your skills and effectiveness again. We're confident that you will find improvement through the utilization of the processes and exercises in this book. Enjoy the journey!

*   *   *

Introduction

CAUTION: Using the material and techniques outlined in this book will fundamentally change your life.

This book and the material in it were born from a desire to make no more cold calls. Pounding the pavement, dialing for dollars, knocking on doors? No thank you. This is field research you are reading. It is battle tested and approved for general use. Best of all, it is applicable in every day life as well as business situations.

It has taken the authors on an incredible journey from cold calls and marketing plans of old to a new year of no cold calling and selling more than the year before. The process has been used to secure a very important job for one of the authors that centers around networking and making things happen based on the principles and ideas outlined herein. We are two guys just like you who decided that there had to be a better way and we set out to find it. Together we have networked and built a very successful speaking and consulting business.

So never fear; the ideas here work. They are real, powerful and effective if you use them. If you don't use them then please give this book to someone else after you read it. The ideas may not all be original and we will give credit to the masters who have gone before us where credit is due. If you are one that deserves credit and we neglected you please forgive us and let us know so we can give you credit next time around. Sit back relax and enjoy the show.

Networking is **work** but it is a lot more fun than making cold calls and the money is better too.

*   *   *

Chapter 1 – Networking

Did you know that you were networking today? Maybe you referred a friend to a local dry cleaners or auto mechanic. Perhaps you helped someone find a store in the mall when asked, or maybe you just conveyed well wishes from one friend to another. These are all forms of networking. Everyone is networking all the time. Whether for business, charity or friendship, networking is a part of all our lives.

Networking is and has been one of the most relied upon ways for small and large businesses alike to build their business base. Networking is cost

> *A Networking Plan is essential to networking success.*

effective, easily measured for success or failure, and often times fun! Sadly for many of us, networking becomes a chore and a bore. This happens when we fail to understand exactly what it is that we are trying to accomplish with our networking efforts.

Most everyone knows that a customer that comes to us through word of mouth promotion is very likely to be one who will become a loyal customer and one who will send us future referrals. But did you know that a potential contributor to your favorite charity will donate more money more often if they have a personal or networked relationship with that charity? Even our relationships are enhanced when we are referred to a potential new friend. As the saying goes "any friend of yours is a friend of mine". What most people don't know is that they can control to a large extent the quantity and quality of the referrals they receive.

Networking is simply the process of expanding our relationship (business or personal) footprint for the purposes of spreading our message. Whether you're single and looking for a mate or whether you're the President of Big Bucks Incorporated, you are continually spreading your message, which gets spread again and again for you through your network and the networks of those you don't even know. It has been said that there are six degrees of separation between any one person and another on the planet. When put in those terms, it can get down right scary! After all, once our message leaves us, we have no control over how it is communicated or interpreted. This is why it is vital to have a networking plan.

A Networking Plan

Your networking plan should contain three main components:

1. A plan for your direct networking efforts.
2. A plan for your indirect networking efforts.
3. A plan for your referral efforts.

A plan for your direct networking efforts will include how and when you will be networking. While we are networking all the time, it is important to *plan* certain networking sessions. These will include breakfasts, luncheons, after hours, and meetings that you will attend regularly. Participation in these events on a regular basis gives you the opportunity to prove your reliability while meeting those people you will find desirable to network with. Occasionally these events will provide direct sales but the big win is in the networking with each participant's network, the people not present at the events. This is the greatest opportunity to expand your sphere of influence since you will be using the recommendation of others to meet new prospects and clients. This process is discussed in depth in this book.

At such events it is common that you will have the opportunity to give your "sixty second commercial" (what we call an MNM – Magical Networking Moment). Often it is in a structured process where each person will have the floor and all will be heard, while other times you will be interacting one on one with people new to you. These networking events provide outstanding opportunities to hone your skills in the delivery of your message. Whether it is the chance meeting in a restaurant or through a networking event, your message must be planned and crafted in such a way that people will feel compelled to know you and your product and that eventually they will feel just as compelled to promote you and your product to their sphere of influence.

It seems to be a common thread in structured networking events that they occur (for the most part) on our own time. Breakfasts, luncheons, after hours, structured networking events happen more often than not at times when we are not "on the clock". This presents two problems. First, our attitude is of a more relaxed nature. We seem to forget that we are here for a reason and understandably so. We're entitled to relax a bit, and since this is our time, shouldn't we be relaxing? The second problem that occurs is that since we've relaxed we often find our efforts less than fruitful. This leads us to mistakenly believe that networking doesn't work. Nothing could be further from the truth.

We must remember that although this is "our time", we have chosen to invest our time in networking to make our work time more effective. In doing so we will be reaping the rewards of less stress, more happiness, and more time for ourselves, and of course ultimately more money. This is a pretty good investment in deed, if we make the proper investment to reap the reward.

> *We are networking all the time. Create a networking plan to maximize your networking efforts.*

*   *   *

Chapter 2 - Starting to Network

We all arrive at networking the same way. We drive. No seriously, we arrive at it because we hear or have first hand knowledge that it is a fantastic way to turbo charge our business. It has the ability to move us from so-so to significance. So let's start where networking starts.

You have chosen your event carefully for the large number of people or for the specific type of people that you are certain will be there. The key with any networking event is the same as fishing. Go where the fish are if you want to catch fish.

Now you have arrived and you turn off your car and begin the final touches of preparation for the event. You check your hair in the mirror. You adjust your tie if you're a man and touch up your make up if you're a woman. As with all things, first impressions are important and you want to make a good one. So you adjust and primp and know that you look great. Now you're ready. Well almost. Do you have your cards? Do you have your name badge? If not grab both and then get going.

Cell Phone

Do you bring your cell phone or leave it in the car? That is a tough one. If it rings and you answer it you will look important and that may gain me some points with those networking. It's always good to look important. But on the other hand if you are in the middle of a great connection and it rings it could blow the whole thing if you answer it. What to do? What to do?

Authors Opinion....

Leave it in the car. If you must carry it, make it silent and never look at it when it vibrates. Get alone and see who called if you must but never let anyone know that it rang. There are very few if any calls that are so important that a few minutes delay until you can get alone will be too long. The message you send to everyone in the room and especially those who are in front of you is: "I know who you are. I don't know who is calling me. But I'm certain whoever is on the phone is more important to me than you are".

Now you're on your way you are confident and ready for the event. You have plenty of business cards. If you don't have cards it's really tough to network. Business cards are your ticket to success and you should look at them that way. They should be clear and concise with your contact information on them and your business clearly recognizable. If you want to be safe, take about twenty cards. More looks like you're a shotgunner (and we will talk about how that is one style but perhaps not the style you want to adopt).

Success in any networking endeavor is the ability to control those things we can control and to anticipate those that we cannot, incorporating a contingency plan for the unexpected. This section focuses on those things we can do to eliminate unnecessary concerns before we utter the first word. Being prepared physically as well as mentally with a verbal message of clarity and power will equip you for massive success, unlimited confidence, and abundant self worth. Seems like a good investment of time to learn how, doesn't it?

Your physical appearance and how you carry yourself will dramatically affect the effectiveness of your message. According to numerous studies, more than 75% of all communication is non-verbal. So while it is critical that we have crafted the right message verbally, it is essential to being heard that we have crafted the right message physically. What's this?

We're not suggesting that if you didn't win a beauty contest in school that you are doomed in networking. But with more than 75% of our communication being non-verbal it is easy to understand why we listen to people we find attractive. Physical beauty however can be a detriment if it is not incorporated into a useful physical and verbal message.

Based upon our formula for success – controlling those things we can, let's look at the physical aspects of networking that we can control. For the purposes of this study we'll examine a typical networking breakfast or luncheon; however the rules can be adapted to most any networking situation.

First let's remember that we're about to be on stage. We wouldn't go on stage in the wrong costume would we? If you are a professional and you dress casually to attend a networking event, you might be communicating a "casual" approach to your business which may be fine for some, but many people will not take you seriously if you don't appear to take your appearance seriously. The exception to this rule is when your business calls for casual dress or even a casual uniform: mechanics, plumbers, electricians or carpenters who have physical jobs requiring them to "get dirty" would not be taken seriously unless they looked the part unless of course they are the business owner who has expanded beyond doing the work themselves. Regardless of the attire, it is vital that you arrive clean and well-groomed. If you have taken time out from physical work to attend a business building networking event, take a few more moments to make certain that you look your best – even if your best is just well groomed in a dirty work uniform!

This brings us to an important point. One thing that we must endeavor to do is to appear in control of our world. No one wants to refer business to someone who doesn't appear to "have it together".

Having it together means that you are neat and well-groomed, dressed appropriately for the occasion, on time and fully prepared.

The first step to appearing to have it together is to allow for enough time. Too often people will arrive to networking events late or leave early not realizing that they have sent a critically flawed message to the rest of the crowd: "You're not important enough to me to plan to arrive on time and to allot the time necessary to really be here with you". People who are late generally disrupt the flow of the group and the effectiveness of the person or persons they interrupt with their late arrival. They appear to not care about others.

If your networking event

> *Failure is often traced*
> *back to a*

starts at noon, your calendar should be cleared thirty minutes before (plus the travel time necessary) and at least fifteen minutes after. The thirty minutes before allows you enough time to gather your thoughts, obtain your give-aways (promotional materials, gifts, business cards), care for your appearance, allot for unexpected time delays and some personal networking time before everyone arrives. The fifteen minutes after allows for personal networking time after the event. This time is sufficient to schedule an appointment with one or two individuals to have personal time with them at a more appropriate date and time.

Arriving early gives you the opportunity to examine the room. Early arrival also gives you a chance to test your voice in the room. Standing on one side of the room and saying hello to someone on the other side will allow you the opportunity to see just how far your voice will carry in any room. Acoustics will vary widely from room to room and will be dependent upon the floor covering, wall covering, and number of windows, open areas, furniture and number of people in the room.

Perhaps the biggest benefit you will obtain from early arrival will be the ability to control where you will sit and whom you will sit near. At networking breakfasts and luncheons, seating is essential to success. Whether it is a concern for comfort or for access to a particular individual, where you sit will have a huge impact on how well your networking is working. The two things to consider when choosing your seating are: 1) access and 2) neighbors.

Access is the ability to easily move in and out of our location and with few exceptions it is the most important thing to consider when choosing a seating location. Ideally you should choose a chair or booth location that allows you to get up and move around without requiring others to do so. Therefore if the choice is a booth, remain standing until someone else chooses to sit and then ask to sit beside them (on the outside). This allows you to control your environment. Unless the opportunity to sit next to

> *Your first choice in any networking event is standing – unless of course you are eating a meal. Then the best choice is at a table on the outermost seat.*

someone you've been trying to meet presents itself, choosing a booth is rarely a good choice. Booths allow for only limited interaction and they restrict all seated there to the company at hand. Tables, if available, offer a far more productive opportunity with regard to networking.

When choosing a seat at a table, avoid chairs that are against a wall since most times these will not afford the ability to get up and move around at will. The exceptions to this rule are chairs that are at the corner of or the end of the table. Again, you want to be able to move around without inconveniencing others. When faced with a long table of chairs, personal preference comes into play. Clearly if you sit in the middle, you will have access to more people since if you sit on the end there will be no one to your right or left as there would be in the middle. However, from the end you have a clearer vision of those at the table and can access them visually, which will often give you the ability to approach these people for a personal meeting after the open session. In any case, unless the beginning of the meeting is imminent, reserve your seat with your belongings and remain standing, greeting others until the beginning of the session. The purpose of attendance is to network. Networking is rarely done from a seat alone at a table.

Neighbors present opportunities and risks when it comes to networking. Of course if you arrive early (which we suggest) you will undoubtedly utilize the opportunity to choose a seat of advantage without knowing who your neighbor will be. But if you arrive in a facility and all the most advantageous seats are already reserved, your neighbor now becomes the most important consideration. If you have done your homework, there are at least one or two people you've come to this meeting with the explicit plan to get to know a little better. Seek those individuals out and sit as close to them as possible. If this is not an option, we suggest that you sit next to someone you do not know, or don't know very well. This will facilitate discussion that will be new and potentially fruitful. You are already having productive discussion with those you know, why sit next to them and use this time to discuss old business when you could be developing new relationships and new business. New relationships and new business is the purpose of attending the meeting.

> *Networking is rarely done from a seat alone at a table.*

Once we have chosen our seating, we must be prepared for all things that will occur prior to them occurring. If this group stands for invocation or a pledge to the flag, you must be prepared for that formality. When orders are being taken by the wait staff, nothing is more disrupting than the one person who hasn't decided what they will order. It also shows everyone at the table that you can't make decisions or at least you aren't prepared when you should be. Therefore, make certain to use the time prior to prepare for ordering. When asked by a waiter or waitress for your order, give them the courtesy of your attention with eye contact and use their name if they are wearing a name badge. Pause to ask them how their day is going, just a little something to humanize the interaction. It tells people you value others. It will also make you feel better, just try it.

The obvious exception to this suggestion is if orders are taken during the sixty second commercials of others. It is best when faced with this type of networking event to have your food and drink preference written on a small slip of paper that you can hand to the wait staff. Make certain to anticipate questions like "well done" or "cream and sugar with coffee" to avoid unnecessary discussion.

> *Remember that the interaction is all about the other person. There is a time for small talk, but let the other person do that. That's what makes you a great conversationalist.*

Now that we've arrived early, chosen our seating and ordered our meal, what should be done next? If the structure of the meeting is open networking, you should do so. Don't waste time discussing things that mean little to the people there. Rarely does anyone really want to hear about your weekend if they are "networking". There is a time for friendly discussion to be sure but make certain that you allow others this privilege. People think about themselves first, last and always so allow them the opportunity to tell you about them. This will be valuable later in the relationship since not only will you know more about them, they will find you to be a great conversationalist (since you listen more than talk).

A networking event is rarely a good time to give a sales pitch. Often we find the people who are networking by pitching to be pushy and unpleasant to be around. Remember, this is networking not selling. People at networking events are not anticipating doing business with you; they are anticipating YOU doing business with THEM. Therefore we need to remember to listen more than we talk and to use this networking time to learn about the others in the group and plan for meeting those with whom we choose to personally network with later.

Perhaps no point in networking more misunderstood than the simple fact that Power Networkers rarely wish to do business with a particular individual. Are there people at networking events that Power Networkers wish to have as customers? Of course there are.

But the Power Networker understands the simple truth that the ultimate power in networking is to have people promoting you to their sphere of influence, using their relationship with others to draft new business for you. The Power Networker not only wants your business and access to your relationship base, he or she wants YOU to be an advocate in that relationship base for him or her.

> *Be on time and courteous. Use open time to network – remember that your goal is to develop a relationship with another who will open their sphere of influence to you.*

*   *   *

Chapter 3 - Networking Styles

Who am I and where do I fit in? A common question in many walks of life that presents itself here in the world of networking as well. This is a good topic to explore. Once you find out who you are and where you fit in you can start to make some decisions. You can then decide if you like who you are and where you fit in? Does it help you meet your objectives? It is important to remember that, regardless of your love of or distaste for your position, you are lucky because you are not stuck there. You can decide to make the changes to achieve the results you are looking to achieve.

Some of us are trying to get to a destination on a train that has never left the station, and others are headed in the opposite direction and are hoping that just somehow things will turn around and we will arrive. In networking it is no different. You need first to know where you are and what kind of train you're traveling on to determine how and when you will arrive. So let's get started.

There are four styles of networkers we will discuss. Some may argue that there are in fact five since we do not discuss the "wall flower". The wall flower is one who comes to networking events, talks to know one, literally hugs the wall of the room, and then leaves. This person does not have a "networking personality" and therefore cannot be considered a networking style. It is as if they are not even in the room. Adding this type of attendee to the "networking styles" would require including everyone who doesn't participate or even show up. The wall flower is essentially the equivalent of one who doesn't come to the even and therefore does not require discussion.

Therefore, we submit that there are only four styles. There may be blends of each of these and perhaps there may be more, but in our experience most people land fairly squarely in one of these four styles. Remember that your goal is first to find out where you are and then to determine if you want to stay there or change styles. The choice is up to you.

Social Light

The first style we will discuss is the SOCIAL LIGHT, not because it's the best but simply because one must come first and this is often how many people get started into networking. Some of them never grow into anything more because this first style is soooooo comfortable.

With the **SOCIAL LIGHT** Networker, the emphasis is on the social part of networking. This networker is heavy on the "social" and light on the "networking", thus the name.

This is the person that hangs out with their close friends, the people that they already know, like and trust people from their own office or people that they are dating or want to date. This is like a little networking party. It looks a lot like a Friday or Saturday evening night out without all the other business people around. Often times it's a group of guys that stands around and talks about all the cute girls, or vice versa. Sometimes two groups will collide and you have a larger group of co-ed social light networkers. While they are always talking it is rarely about business. Social Lights always have something in common that bonds them together. That bond is almost always a non-business related topic.

They occasionally will meet someone they don't know but it is not very common. They never get any business from the networking event but when they are asked about networking it gets positive reviews. When the boss asks about the event it was always great and lots of people where there, and when friends ask they are told; "too bad you missed it". Tom won a door prize. It bears repeating that this crowd is big on the social and light on the networking.

Now that's not all bad as we all need to start somewhere and this is usually the place. These folks need to meet the host of the event so that they can meet some new people by introduction.

Generally speaking they are great conversationalist but don't have a high level of skill in networking. If introduced to someone new they will have the ability to carry on a conversation even if they are uncomfortable. These people are usually very "social".

How do we improve their networking skill and move them along in the networking process so that they make more money and get better results? Well hang on a

> *The Social Light networker is heavy on the "social" and light on the "networking".*

minute and lets look at the next style of networking and see if there is a logical progression or any progression at all for that matter.

SHOTGUN

She or he is an overly confident type or one that simply overly compensates for the lack of confidence by an exceptionally large amount of activity. We call them the SHOTGUN Networker. They come to each meeting the same way as everyone else. They prepare and make sure that they look good adjusting the tie or the makeup before they leave the car. They make the cell phone decisions too. The one thing that they are sure of is the business card. They've got lots of them. This is a powerful weapon in the hands of the shotgun networker. Everyone's card holds with it the power to make another shot at getting business.

It's another chance to wound some unsuspecting networker with his or her product or service. Today is the day. This person is often from the old school of selling. It's strictly a numbers game. If he or she can hand out 100 business cards tonight then WOW; it will have been a great success.

> *And off they go, to shotgun the 100 business cards to anyone and everyone. Everyone will get the Shotgun Networker's card*

The pitch is the same over and over and over. Hi my name is Shotgun Sam (short for Samuel or Samantha) I am with ABC Co we do ABC better than anyone does ABC in the whole world. We are fast and cheap and our customers always love us. Give me a call sometime. See ya round. (Some of you are laughing right now because you know Sam and have a card for every meeting he was at with you last year.)

The hand off of his or her card is made and then; off they go to the next victim. We say victim because that is often how the person receiving the card feels. "Oh my, what am I going to do? I guess I will just stand here and let this happen. It has to end soon." The good news is that it does. There is no way that they will remember Shotgun Sam until the next event where they will try without success to avoid the interaction again.

Shotgun Sam gets famous. Actually the proper description would be notorious. He or she has the dubious distinction of being known by everyone and yet few will do business with him or her unless they absolutely have to.

Back at the office Shotgun Sam raves about the event and how many great people got his card. The food was good but that is secondary to the primary purpose. Get rid of my business cards. After a few events the request for more cards goes to the boss and all the networking is given as the reason for the refill. The boss doesn't know any better until now and orders more cards for Shotgun Sam to glad hand out to the next crowd of people he or she comes across.

Clearly, this is not how you want to run your networking. Shotgun Sam isn't getting any cards in return. So he or she changes her pitch, simply adding a few phrases such as: Can I get one of your cards?

We know you thought that there were more phrases coming but no. Shotgun Sam simply needs a stack of cards for his or her desk to fill up the empty box that he or she asked the boss to restock. When the boss comes by, he or she can point to the box and say "I met all those people last month". The boss walks away and orders the additional cards and is impressed by the volume of activity the individual is doing.

If Shotgun Sam gets really bold he may say 'I'll call you sometime". This at first strikes fear into the heart of the listener but after a few networking events and weeks with no call the fear goes away. For Sam the fear is always there. Why? No connection was made. If he or she breaks through that fear and actually makes a phone call, the phone call goes just like the introduction and business card exchange.

Hi my name is Shotgun Sam I am with ABC Co we do ABC better than anyone does ABC in the whole world. We are fast and cheap and our customers always love us. I met you at the networking event last week. Give me a call sometime. See ya round.

The connection never gets made and business doesn't get done and networking doesn't work. This is the primary reason that the Chamber networking events are called business card exchanges.

In our investigation of the networking styles, we have moved from the "social" aspect of networking to the work part of things but still there is no business. That's just no good.

MR. "BIG" or MS. "BIG" HUNTER

So let us move along and see what comes next. Mr. "Big" Bill or Ms. "Big" Barb HUNTER are people who are really networking. They show up at the event just like everyone else. Appearance is critical for this crowd. They must look perfect; a 10 at every turn. No hair out of place and nothing missing - 100% perfect or close to it. The cell phone issue is critical for these folks because Mr. "Big" or Ms. "Big" is powerful and important. Does the cell phone go or does it stay in the car? While they agonize over this question, our answer is always the same.

They show up early and stay late and have one singular purpose for the event: Meeting Mr. "Big" or Ms. "Big". So just who is this person and why is it so important to meet them? Here it is, there big shot a chance to change everything, to meet that person of such incredible influence and power that just contact with

> *Mr. or Ms. Big Hunter might as well be wearing a safari hat! The quest that they are on is just like the hunting of big game.*

them could catapult there career, sales effort or whatever business they are in to the top in their field. Mr. Big or Ms. Big is the person everyone wants to know and to be known by them. Typically these people are at the top of their profession or field or have a powerful position that affords them the title of Mr. Big or Ms. Big.

They are tough to hunt though. They sometimes don't show up and our Hunter goes home hungry. This networker never eats and never drinks, because it might be just upon taking a bite or drink that the opportunity presents itself for the kill. These people are annoyed by Shotgun Sam because nothing will drive potential attendees (including Mr. Big or Ms. Big) away faster than Shotgun Sam since he or she let the big game see his or her gun! No one is more focused than our hunter.

When Mr. Big or Ms. Big shows up they always have an entourage and it continues to grow as the event goes. They know everyone and everyone knows them. That is why they are so valuable that one would actually hunt them.

So let's talk about the hunt. Our hunter must be careful to be seen but not too much, so as not to scare Mr. "Big" or Ms. "Big". Often times they will be spotted and then Mr. "Big" or Ms. "Big" feels like they are being stalked. Male "Big" hunters must be especially careful hunting Ms. "Big" so they don't get the wrong idea. Business and pleasure mixing is a tricky game and not one for the networking events unless you are very, very skilled. When the opportunity presents itself (and sometimes this can take several hours or even several meetings) they pounce on their prey and let them have it.

The pitch is very similar to Shotgun Sam, hi my name is Happy Hunter I am with ABC Co we do ABC better than anyone in the whole world. We are fast and cheap and our customers always love us. Give me a call sometime. See ya round. It spills of the tongue like it was rehearsed and in fact it was. They always give and get a card and sometimes will even make the follow up telephone call. They have bagged Mr. "Big" or Ms. "Big".

> *People often fail to remember that it is called net<u>working</u>. Successful networkers <u>work</u> at being successful networkers.*

Often times they find that this person who they thought was so powerful and influential just simply isn't. Rarely do they conduct business with them. When they do make the telephone call the pitch is the same and they get brushed off by the gate keeper or voice mail. Networking didn't work for our Hunter either. The connection never gets made, business doesn't get done and networking doesn't work.

Now wait a minute. If all these people are failing at networking why do so many people rave about it? And if all these people are doing it wrong, how is done it right? You will find our final networker to have the answers you're looking for. While reading about the techniques will dramatically improve your networking results, participating in real life activities will give you a quantum leap. But where can one "practice" networking? We have two great answers for you.

QBC – Quick Business Connections is a 1.5 hour or longer event limited to 48 people where quick business connections are made and you can test your Power Networking Skill set. By hosting this speed networking program, you control the invited guests, improve you sales teams effectiveness, and facilitate others meeting the right people. This program makes you the hero!

Is Your Networking Working? This workshop is presented as a half day or full day workshop which can be customized for your organization. This intensive yet fun program will arm you and your staff for Power Networking Success.

For further information please call 877-893-1821 or visit www.isyournetworkingworking.com.

Power Networker

Okay - enough talk about Power Networking. Let's tell you what it is and how it works. The Power Networker, like all other networkers, arrives and checks in the mirror. First impressions are important to them too. The cell phone decision is easily made, they are here for business.

> *Life is a game and the sooner we learn that games make work more enjoyable the sooner we start winning more often.*

Business cards are always available and ready, typically in the left hand pocket. It's easy to shake hands and then get a card if they are in the right spot. Ladies your purse works well for this if your attire has no convenient pocket. Name tags are typically like the business card, clear concise and easy to read. Everyone can see at a glance who you are and what you do. Name badges are usually worn on the right side of the chest to direct attention when shaking hands.

The Power Networker shows up early and stays late knowing that you never know who you are going to meet when. They enjoy themselves. Not too much food, very little if any alcohol; after all, this is about business. They always have a game plan.

That's right; a game plan. For them this is networking and it is work, but it is fun and they have made it a game that they play. We know that when we approach any endeavor as a game, we will work harder and pay more to play it than we will work when we are paid. Think about your favorite sporting activity and what it costs you and what you put into it as far as effort. If you did that on your job you would be wildly successful. If you're reading this and you are wildly successful you know what I am talking about. Life is a game and the sooner we learn that games make work more enjoyable the sooner we start winning more often.

So what is the Power Networkers game plan? It is simple but effective. They come with the express written intent to meet five to seven people; more or less depending upon the size of the event, the number of attendees and the duration. People in the other networking styles think meeting five to seven people is no problem. What do the other networking style folks think when they are told that Power Networkers want to meet between five and seven people?

Social Light – Tom, Sally, Tim, Linda, George, Bruce, Peggy and Matt are going to be there - got that covered.

Shotgun – only five to seven? What good does that do? That's hardly even worth going. Give me 100 or nothing.

Mr. "Big" and Ms. "Big" Hunter – I only need one good one to make the difference and I have already picked them out, I just need them to show.

It may surprise you that of all the networking styles our Big Hunter friend is closest to the truth. As we begin to implement our Power Networking Game Plan we discover that of the five to seven target, if we meet just one or two really good contacts it could make all the difference. The underlying theme of the Power Networker goes back to what we talked about earlier. All things being equal, people will do business with those people that they know, like and trust. This is what we are working on and it goes something like this.

Hi my name is Glen, what is yours?

Well, Brenda what do you do?

How long have you been in the advertising business?

What got you started in advertising?

Who are some of the people you do business with?

And on and on and on, question after question after question, about them. The key here is to listen. Listen to what they say so you can understand who they are and what they are about. Dr. Wayne Dyer says listen with the intent to understand not to respond. Dale Carnegie says that you will be known as a brilliant conversationalist if you learn to listen to the other person talk about themselves, after all it is their favorite subject. Now what does that do for the Power Networker? It makes them likeable, one of the three keys for more business (know, like and trust). It also makes them known, another of the three keys for more business (know, like and trust). It's about relationships, business relationships. That is what Networking is all about.

> *All things being equal, people will do business with those people that they know like and trust.*

So you have talked a lot about them. You really have asked a lot of open ended questions and listened. You listened to get to know them and you listened to determine if they are someone you would like to get to know more. You are searching for common ground where you might be able to help them out. Yes, I know you thought that networking was all about you increasing your business, well keep reading we are getting there.

If you determine that you are interested in going further then exchange cards. Talk with them further, more questions of course. Remember to let them know what you do, but not too much as you want the conversation to be primarily about them. Then just before parting you want to ask them a final and very important question. It is what we call **the million dollar question.**

This is a question that they most likely will have never heard before and you will get some interesting looks when you ask it. It goes something like this: Debra *if I were to come across someone in my daily business that could use your services or benefit from your product, how would I recognize them and what would be the best way to put them in touch with you?*

<u>WOW!</u> That is a powerful question. One of the keys to it's power is that it has been asked at the right time. If asked after the relationship has begun to grow (through your thoughtful questioning and careful listening as outlined previously) you will get responses. So listen carefully, very carefully and then part with some version of "it was nice to meet you" or "I would love to call you sometime" and leave.

When you leave, get your pen and make notes on the back of their card about the conversation and the answer to the question. Do it immediately.   Be certain to mark the front of their card as well to remind you that information is on the back and this is NOT a Shotgun Sam card. While you may have the memory of an elephant (we all believe we do) we do forget from time to time although we may not like to admit it. If you don't write it down you may forget it. So take the time and make the effort to jot a note or two as a reminder. Then and only then are you ready to meet someone else.

If the first person introduces you to someone else you have to remember to write on both cards before you continue on. Make certain that you note the connection between the two individuals as well. This information is going to be incredibly valuable in part two of your networking game plan. It is better to write the information down in front of the person and be certain you have it than to plan to write it down and forget to. Your currency is information. This is what you will purchase trust and ultimately new business with.

The next person you meet you will treat the same way. With questions and respect, listening to what they have to say and discovering if there is a QBC – a Quick Business Connection.

Meeting people with this intentionality is only to see if it makes sense to go further and build a relationship. These chance meetings sometimes result in immediate business and if that occurs so much the better. Then get back to the game plan. QBC – Quick Business Connections take about five to ten minutes they are a key strategy in the power networkers game plan. Now you know why you can only make five to seven connections at a given event. That's about an hour or so worth of work and your event time frame may not allow for a whole lot more than that. So show up early and stay late and implement your game plan to win at the game of networking.

Power networkers do important things after the meeting as well that set them apart from other networkers. The make the calls to those five to seven people that they met. They invite them for a cup of coffee or lunch so that they can learn more about them, remember: know like and trust. They prepare for these mini networking events by researching the other guys company so that you know more about them. They work to bring a referral to the first meeting. If you can pull this off then you will see your sales increase in a big way. You may be wondering how giving someone else a referral for their business could increase your business in a big way. Well we will talk about that more in the Art of the Referral section of this book.

Power networkers are careful to remember (via the aid of notes on the back of a card) the things they learned about the person they are networking with. This shows that you really care, and you do or else you wouldn't be going through the effort to build a network. You would just go out and make more cold calls. This process is time consuming and often time's people get caught up in the time invested before they realize results. Let's just briefly touch on that here. We will expand on it in the sowing and reaping (Art of the Referral) portion of this text.

If you planted some tiny seeds and when they popped their little heads out of the dirt and sprouted that first leaf, would you then yank them from the ground and say that farming doesn't work? I think not. That is precisely where you are at this stage in your game plan. The relationship has just begun to bud and you need to tend to it and nurture it before you can expect the fruit. So hang in there, keep working the plan and you will see the results that you're looking for.

> **All too often people give up on their efforts before they have a chance to grow. Success happens when you plant a seed and nurture it to maturity – then we can harvest.**

You see this is not a sometimes thing we are talking about here. This isn't a maybe this will work for you maybe it won't deal. This is a 100% guaranteed bona fide, tried and true results based game plan. The only reason it will fail is if you fail to work it. Even that famous salesman who calls saying; "You wouldn't want to buy something would you?" sells something, so stick to the plan. It works and it works well. We all know people who have implemented this plan with such success that they have given up cold calling completely. This author is just one of them. Perhaps you like cold calling, perhaps you don't, but if you're this far along in this book then we suspect you are looking for a better way. Congratulations, You found it.

So the questions are simple, where are you when it comes to networking? Where do you want to be when it comes to networking?

Being a Social Light is a fine place to start. Shot gunning is a lot of action for certain, and hunting is clearly more focused, but let us take the best of all three. Let's fine tune them, rev them up like an Italian sports car and let get networking with a Powerful Power Networking Game Plan that makes business sense because it makes business happen.

How do you change? How do you grow? Well that's where we come in. The tools are here in this book for you to use and implement. Just like the road in front of your house, it can take you just about anywhere you imagine. However, if you never leave the house you know what happens.

We offer networking coaching as a supplement to this book. It is effective and focused on achieving results. So when you're ready or if you want some extra help, please send an email to: networking@inspirationagents.com or call 941-870-4070 or visit www.isyournetworkingworking.com for details. The greatest teams in history owe considerable credit to the coach as well as the team. Great coaches get more from the players of the game than the players thought they had inside.

*   *   *

Chapter 4 - Building the Machine

How to Develop an Effective MNM (Magical Networking Moment)

You have the proper stature and you're working your game plan but when it comes time to deliver your pitch it sounds just like that: a pitch. Have you ever heard a pitch coming in off the mound, it sounds like a lot of moving air then **POW**; the pitch hits the glove and its over, simply to be repeated again. It's powerful, but only effective when controlled and directed with a desired result.

> *Networking is about generating more business – so think like marketers think. You must be prepared to present.*

We want you to do more than pitch. we want for you to pitch with intention, with control and with desired results. What we wish for you to do is to ***present***. Think of delivering something that is more along the lines of a commercial. Why do all those big multi-million dollar companies pay millions of dollars for seconds of time for their commercials in the Super Bowl? Because commercials work, they sell, they get more business. You should remember that networking is about generating more business. So let's have an effective and exciting commercial that causes the viewer to remember you and your product and ultimately causes them to refer and buy.

We admit that is easier said than it is done. What do I include and what do I leave out? Do I tell them where we are located? My phone number? What about promotions, or office hours? There are literally countless ways to present a commercial. What really works? What will people buy? First, let's get started with the purpose of MNM's (Magical Networking Moments).

The purpose of a MNM (also known as a sixty-second commercial) is to convey to the listener the value you can bring to their sphere of influence in such a way that they are compelled to take action for you. In other words, people are moved to action on your behalf. They either buy your product or service or tell someone else about your product or service. In either case you get what you came for and that is more business.

So let's take a moment to think about the most memorable commercials we have ever seen. Do you remember Mean Joe Green in the Coca Cola commercial with the little kid in the football tunnel? How about the Polar Bears drinking Coca Cola? Remember the little old lady in the Wendy's commercial "Where's the beef?" What about the little Chihuahua in the Taco Bell commercial "Yo Quiero Taco Bell"? Dell's "dude your getting a dell." There are tons more.

How about some old ones? Winston tastes good like a cigarette should. See the USA in a Chevrolet. We remember them and some of us have never seen them. These last few examples have been off the air for years. What does that say about the power of a commercial? It lasts, it makes an impression, and it moves us to the point that it shapes our world and how we view it.

We are not suggesting that your MNM (Magical Networking Moment) needs to do all these things but remember; it's SHOWTIME! So live it up deliver a memorable performance.

Your message must be clear and individual focused. People must feel that you are talking with them and that your product solves a problem or meets a need that they have or someone they know may have. You need to be personable and let them know about real people that have been helped or who have used your product or service.

> *Your MNM should be crafted in such a way that the listener thinks one of two things: "I need that" or "I know someone who needs that".*

What do we relate to in the great commercials? We can see ourselves in them, or we get a feeling from them that we want so we go and buy the product for the feeling that we want. So we relate to the things we can see ourselves doing in them. Involve your audience. Ask questions, give answers, deliver tips; do something to set you apart from the others in the crowd.

It is important to remember that often less is more. Often we feel compelled to include more information than the listener can retain or cares about. You must remember to make it compelling and memorable. The key question to answer from the listeners' perspective is: what's in it for me? Why should they listen and what are they going to get? Is your commercial visually interesting? Is it audibly interesting? Is it analytically interesting? What is interesting about it? How do you involve the audience's senses? Remember that we all have five senses and the more we can touch in the MNM, the more powerful it will be.

Just think how your favorite commercial would be without the sound? Or perhaps you could just hear it and not see the visuals? Would it loose any of its impact? Clearly the answer is yes and the same holds true for you.

When it comes to compelling the audience to take action on our behalf by either buying our product or service or referring someone else to buy our product or service we can chose the carrot or the stick method of motivation. The carrot or the stick refers to how one might get a donkey to move. You might hold a carrot in front of the donkey, creating a sense of potential gain or you might strike the donkey with a stick from behind creating pain (a sense of loss). Craft your message by creating a sense of loss if they don't take action (this is the stick) or by creating a sense of gain if they do (this is the carrot). It is difficult to do both. Many of you are going to be "hard wired" positively and would never consider using the negative (stick) method. Like you, when asked if the glass is half full or half empty, we see the glass a 100% full; half water and half air. But when it comes to your MNM remember the power of loss and the simple fact that most people are motivated more by loss avoidance than potential gain.

> *You are guaranteed success in networking if you develop a plan and decide in advance to pay the price necessary to achieve the results you desire.*

The sense of loss is aligned with the sense of pain. We won't go too deep here because there are countless people who have written more extensively on the subject and know considerably more about it than we do. What those experts tell us is that we will typically do more to avoid pain than we will to gain pleasure. Translate that to your commercial. What are the people going to miss out on if they don't take action? What pain does your product or service solve? Figure this out and your half way home. A little later on we will walk you through the exercise of creating an effective MNM, and it will be exercise. It is work and just like the gym you have to exercise your commercial or it gets weak and flabby and can't do the heavy lifting that networking requires.

Now let's back up and look at the pleasure side of the equation. It too is powerful and effective so it's a good idea to look at the positive pleasure side of your product or service. What great pleasure will I get from using your dry cleaning business? Massage therapy? Attorney? CPA? Etc. Here again determine what this is and your more than half way home.

Why do we keep saying more than half way home? If you figure out the key thing shouldn't you be further along than just half way? Well not really. Remember that it is SHOWTIME and just like your favorite commercial without the sound or with out the sights if it is not said properly even though the words are right the message can be lost. Let us explain.

Scene 1: Mom is calling for little Johnny. Johnny, come here, in a calm voice with love and anticipation. It's going to be good for Johnny to come and get a hug or a kiss or some other pleasurable experience from Mommy.

Scene 2: Mom is calling for little Johnny. Johnny, COME here, in a loud strong voice signaling a warning. It's going to be good for Johnny to come and avoid the danger Mommy spots.

Scene 3: Mom is calling for little Johnny. Johnny, come HERE. In a loud, stern voice of reprimand. It's going to be good for Johnny to obey and come but he may be in big trouble when he gets there because it sounds like he has done something Mom doesn't approve of.

Scene 4: Mom is calling for little Johnny. Johnny, come here in a soft voice with out any inflection or emphasis. Mom is simply tired of calling little Johnny and she really doesn't expect him to come at all and that is why her attitude is so nonchalant.

You see there are many ways to say it. So when it comes to your MNM (Magical Networking Moment), think about how you want it to sound and what message you want it to convey and let them have it.

Studies have revealed that the vast majority Americans would rather DIE than speak in public. Is it any wonder so many of us struggle when it is our time to shine? No place is this more obvious than when it is our opportunity to deliver our MNM (Magical Networking Moment).

Most often, the opportunity to deliver a MNM (Magical Networking Moment) comes during a gathering of less than thirty people and in a setting that is less than conducive to "performance". This is vital information to be aware of since most often we fail to realize that we are "performing"! It's SHOWTIME! Yet we find

> *Studies continue to show that the vast majority of Americans would rather DIE than speak in public. Public speaking is the greatest fear of the majority of Americans.*

ourselves tucked into a small area of a dining table, between other people who are tucked in as well. Most people aren't really listening either. They are eating, having a sip of coffee, whispering to another next to them, thinking about what they have to say, or virtually anything except for focusing on us. Worse yet, we know this and we begin to think that our moment isn't really that important. Nothing could be further from the truth.

This is our time. Even if the message gets through to no one (which if you follow the instructions in this book it will) it will be remembered by you. Each time you give your MNM (Magical Networking Moment), your sales presentation, or each time you casually tell someone about you, you are marketing to yourself as well. What message are you telling yourself? What subtle statements of doubt, lack of value, and fear are being etched on the canvas of your mind to be relived each time you merely think about (much less talk about) yourself and your business?

> *Successful people smile more – not necessarily because they are successful. They are successful because they smile. Try it.*

These thoughts should make it abundantly clear to you that what you say and how you say it is vital to the overall success and ultimate happiness you will experience in life. After all, how happy can anyone be if they have thoughts during most of the third of their lives dedicated to work that they are inadequate, inept, unappreciated, and ignored?

While this section is dedicated to things you can do to ensure success with your physical body, one factor above all others will determine your success or failure in networking (and in much of life). That factor is your ability to share a smile.

"When you're smilin', the whole world smiles at you" goes the old song and nothing could be more true. Smiling does a world of good, and while a lack of a smile won't always mean that you won't make the connection, a smile will almost always ensure that you will. When you smile, people are naturally attracted to you. Studies show that people who smile are seen as more attractive than those who don't. Other studies have shown that when telemarketers smile while they are on the phone that more sales are made. Our entire voice changes when we smile. Smiling makes us more likable and in return, we feel better about ourselves when we smile.

We suggest that you practice smiling. While it shouldn't, it seems to take effort for many people to remember that they should be smiling. But with practice, you will find that you smile more and when you smile more, you'll feel better about yourself, your work, and your surroundings. People will seem more agreeable. You'll find that you don't feel like you're working as hard as you did before and that good fortune just seems to follow you. And it's no wonder; the world loves to be around good natured people. Good natured people smile a lot. You need to be smiling.

Your Physical Posture Says It All

Remember that your body language is being read all the time. When delivering your MNM (Magical Networking Moment), remember to do the following five things:

1.   Change Position
2.   Pause
3.   Breathe
4.   Lean Forward
5.   Speak Louder

Now the time has come. The sixty second commercials (yours of course will be a Magical Networking Moment) have started. Are you ready? Knowing what to say and how to say it will be executed more easily when you incorporate these five planned physical attributes in your pre-presentation.

Change Position: When it becomes your turn to deliver your sixty second commercial, the first step you must take is to change position. This usually means that you will want to stand up, however if you have found yourself in a less than advantageous seating position that restricts your standing, the best thing to do is to at least change the way that you are seated. This indicates to the "audience" that you are now on stage. You have taken your cue.

> *Here's a great tip. When the person next to you prepares to stand and speak by pushing their chair back, push your chair back at the same time. This way you'll be ready to just stand and deliver – you'll be more at ease not worrying about all the noise your chair would have made. Success is all about being prepared.*

We've all been to luncheons and seen an unprepared individual try to work their way out of a chair to stand, only to bump the table, knock over a glass or drop a knife onto the floor while standing. And of course we've all been the victim of a short presentation just before ours leaving us with a mouth full of food to try to ingest as anxious networkers look on. All of these embarrassing etiquette faux pas can be avoided with proper planning. Prior to changing position, prepare for the eventual movement by quietly pushing your chair back from the table and putting down all utensils when the person next to us pushes their chair back in preparation for standing up. This requires us to be ready to do so while the person next to the person next to us is giving their sixty second commercial.

With the chair pushed slightly (quietly) back from the table and no utensils in hand (and no food in our mouths!) we are prepared when our turn comes to stand gracefully. Standing up brings attention to us. Even if no one else does, if you can stand you should.

Once standing, the next step is to pause. Pausing gives everyone the short moment they need to focus on us. It indicates without saying it that we are about to deliver some very important information. So important in fact that we are going to make certain that everyone is listening. There will be those who will wonder why you aren't speaking, some will even wonder if you've developed stage fright. This works to your advantage since the one thing everyone will do is focus on you. Silence is a powerful attention getter when you aren't expected to be silent. Use the pause to grab the attention of those in the group.

Now, breathe! So often we fail to recognize that we don't prepare our voice with the proper amount of breath to deliver. You wouldn't try to swim the length of the pool without a deep breath would you? Why then would anyone not prepare their voice with enough breath to support the words? Often times we will

> *A deep breath not only powers the voice but also calms the body and mind.*

wonder what it was that was at the end of that sentence, when we would have heard clearly if the speaker had just taken enough air in to support the words coming out.

Breathing deeply also has a very relaxing effect on our bodies. Sufficient oxygen in the bloodstream allows the brain to function at optimal levels, giving our thoughts clarity and our words power. A deep breath relaxes us while heightening our though processes. Not to mention it gives us an added physical indication to the audience that something important is about to occur.

Now, just before the first word, lean slightly forward. Have you ever been in a group of people and someone wanted you to know something important? Do they scream it at you across the group? No! When we want to share really important information, we lean in toward each other to make certain we're heard. Leaning in will give the audience the final cue that what you're about to share is vital, they must listen. Often times a lean forward indicates the sharing of a secret. Everyone loves to know secrets, so lean toward those with whom you are about to share the secret of your business with. They'll love it!

Leaning forward also brings into play an unwritten law of reciprocity. Many times in our lives we take actions because we feel the actions of another require us to return the favor. This is discussed in the section on referrals, but even in our physical lives, we reciprocate that which comes toward us. The next time someone

> *Showtime is no time to have to think about the physical things you will do. You don't think about all the things you do when driving – you just drive. Practice standing, pausing, breathing, leaning in and speaking louder to the point that it becomes second nature. All five should happen simultaneously.*

reaches out to shake hands with you, try to avoid the hand shake. What you will find is that you cannot. It is so natural for you to reciprocate by reaching out and shaking the others hand, you wouldn't dream of doing anything but shake the outstretched hand. The same holds true for all types of physical actions, and when you lean in, many of those at the table will lean in as well. It draws you closer, makes you more human, and gives a sense of closeness that is lacking in most of our lives. Leaning toward those you will speak with will bring you power and best of all, people will like you more!

Now the time has come. The time for the first word out of your mouth - your MNM (Magical Networking Moment). You've planned everything to culminate at this point. The last thing you would want is to not be heard, isn't it? So speak louder than you think in necessary.

So many times people loose the attention they have worked so hard to gain because no one can hear them. They start to speak and someone in the back of the room leans over to another and says "can you hear them?" One leans to another and in an instant, the attention they had is lost. Worse still is the interruption "we can't hear you" screamed from the back of the audience. Don't let this happen to you. Speak loud enough so that even if someone is hard of hearing, they will hear you.

Speaking loudly is often seen as rude in our society, which is why so many people may not speak loudly enough to be heard. From childhood, many of us have been "shushed" into a softer voice. Of course this doesn't work when we are supposed to be heard in an audience. Speaking loud enough to be heard throughout the room indicates to your audience that you are confident in what you say, confident in what your sell, and confident in who you are. Speaking softly indicates that you are unsure of yourself and your product. Clearly, speaking louder than you need to has its benefits. Make certain you are heard.

How do you add some zip to your commercial and make it a little spicy so that people remember it and want to do business with you or send business to you? Earlier we mentioned the five senses and talked briefly about questions, answers and tips. So just how do you incorporate those things into your MNM (Magical Networking Moment)?

We have covered sight with the section above on posture and yet, is it possible that there could be more? You bet. What about props? Not big fancy light sets and stuff like that but simple props that could make you stand out. Here are a couple ideas, and a section for you to jot down some ideas you have for your MNM (Magical Networking Moment). By reading these examples we trust you will begin to have ideas for your particular product or service (and maybe it's even listed here)!

Identity Theft – man dresses up as a woman and talks about how he ordered this that and the other thing using a female name (Citibank made this serious topic funny and capitalized on it)

Spa Owner – puts her hair up before the event and when it's her turn she stands and lets her hair down and gives her head a shake and says "we are all about your image".

Dry Cleaner – wore a white doctors coat and gave out cards inside pill bottles as prescriptions for "stain relief" (a play on pain relief)

Computer Specialist – brought a can of spam and held it up while talking about how bad spam was for your computer

Dance Cruise – performed a few dance moves and talked about how you could get great legs from dancing.

Auto Buyer – brings monopoly money and says if you're interested in saving this then give me a call, or throws it around and says if you're tired of throwing your money away when you buy a car then give me a call.

Magazine Ad Executive – holds a copy of the magazine so people can identify with them

Chiropractor – brought a spine and talked about being out of joint.

Auto Mechanic – brings auto service ads and talks about how untrue they are with $14 oil changes

AFLAC – brings the duck and it squawks AFLAC (by the way they paid millions for that and everyone knows it so use it. If your company has that kind of brand recognition use it - don't ignore it)

Financial Advisor – brought a piggy bank and a CD talked about moving up the investment strategy ladder to a financial advisor

Juice Plus – lady brings her chart of 17 fresh fruits and vegetables and a little capsule a whole days supply in just one small package.

All these are great examples of props. Visual aids that help the audience identify with you and your product. They set you apart and keep you in the mind of the audience just that much longer. They are simple and fun and easily transportable. But most importantly they create a visual impact and touch another of the senses that we all use every day.

What about visuals that don't have a specific tie in to the product or service? They work too. We have seen people stand on chairs to get noticed. We know people who always come in late to get themselves noticed. There are others that we have seen used. Be careful not to go overboard here, getting noticed is one thing getting known is another.

The bottom line is props work and they are incredibly effective. Use them when you can. A part of the exercise we talked about earlier we want you to take a few minutes and think about some props that you could use to make your MNM (Magical Networking Moment) more effective and fun.

On the page that follows, fill in the blanks with potential props you may use during your MNM (Magical Networking

Moment). Consider the things you may use in your sales presentations, your print advertising, or anything that you have that is used to identify you and your product or service.

<u>PROPS to use for my MNM (Magical Networking Moment)</u>
Small things I use that identify my business or profession – Symbols of the end result my clients experience – Pictures that have significance to my business – Mascots created by my company that create branding – The ideas above are ticklers – there will be others to be certain. Jot down your ideas based upon those above and others on the lines that follow. Do this exercise often as your marketing and advertising changes over time.

1._____

2._____

3._____

4._____

5._____

6._____

7._____

The sound of your voice can be very powerful and we talked about being loud enough for people to hear. Now let us take a look at another wonderfully effective way to use our voice and capture the imagination of the listener. Tell me a story. We all love stories, from birth and childhood when they are read to us at nap time and bed time to our teenage years

> *People love stories and can remember them easily. You can get people to relate to using your product or service by telling a story about someone who has used your product or service successfully.*

when we learn to love the movies and the television stories. Stories are everywhere. They are what keep us interested in the soap operas and the reality shows and the books we read.

The Story

Tell success stories; tell how someone used your product and the benefits they enjoyed. Tell how someone used your service and saved their marriage or saved a ton of money on their car insurance. Tell how someone used your product and saw and increase in their sales because they stopped making cold calls and started networking. Tell about the young couple who thought it was too much to start saving or too much to buy the insurance and found out that it really wasn't. We all relate to stories. We can see ourselves in them. So be sure and tell them.

An easy way to construct a story is by using feel, felt and found. Identify the unspoken objections to your product or service; I can't afford it, I don't need it, I use ABC Company's product instead, the list goes on and on. Then, identify someone you have (or someone in your company has) had buy your product or service in spite of the objection. Then tell what they found. Here's an example from our business:

We offer business and personal consulting on networking at a rate of $500.00 per month. For your investment you receive three one hour coaching sessions, a fourth half hour coaching call and unlimited email support. I know how you feel; $500.00 is a lot of money every month to develop your networking skills. Rick felt the same way, but what he found is that the time we spent together, coupled with the assignments he was given each week kept him focused and on task and actually resulted in his making far more each month than the amount he invested in the coaching. What's more, he was able to keep these skills and benefit from them for a lifetime.

We know countless people who have tremendous success stories but are unwilling or afraid to share them or think that we would be disinterested. If they would simply tell the story of how a sales executive used their services to go from being unorganized and having few sales to being highly organized and concentrating on referral business which resulted in more sales, then others might begin to see that it's not just for the super gifted or endowed. Clearly anyone can do this stuff. Stories make us relatable and likeable and all things being equal people do

> *All reputation is earned. Tell the truth without exaggeration. Earn the reputation of being reputable. It will pay great dividends. It's about all three – known, liked, and trusted.*

business with those people that they know, like and trust. So tell us a story about how it worked for someone else.

One clearly, glaringly obvious note about telling stories; tell the truth. If you don't someone will find out and then your hard work building your network of people that know, like and trust you will have been in vain. They WON'T trust you anymore. Trust takes many acts to gain and one act to lose.

Questions Answers and Tips.

These are effective tools to get you noticed using your voice primarily. The really great thing about them is that they are interactive and they get the audience involved. People love to be part of what's going on so engage them and make what's going on about you and them.

Questions and answers are standard fare for just about any game. We talked earlier about how we love to play games and that you should have a networking game plan. This should be part of it. Decide from the start if you want answers or if you want questions. When you want answers you need to think about the questions carefully. There is power in a room full of people answering in unison because they all clearly know the answer to the question. There is no power and in fact there is power and effectiveness lost when no one knows the answer to your questions. So don't make them to tough. The message here is to ask questions that lead to the obvious answers you wish to receive.

Make your questions about your business. Make them fun and quick. Create questions that ultimately tell everyone what it is that you do. Craft them to create word pictures. Make them light and easy and fun. Always make the answer either a show of hands, a yes or no, or some other quick one word or phrase answer.

> *Don't get too clever with the audience. Ask questions to which the answer is obvious. Nothing is more awkward than a question asked that isn't answered the way we intended.*

This conserves time and puts you squarely in control. Make certain the audience knows the way you want to receive your answer. For example: By a show of hands, who wants to make more money this year? Or, (holding your hand in the air to indicate that's what you want them to do) who wants more free time to enjoy it? You get the idea. You can train the audience if you have the time and energy. There is a chiropractor that has been incredibly effective at this. He asks the same question every time. Your body only feels pain for one reason and that is? It's a warning sign. It has become his trademark. Now people recite "it's a warning sign" in unison when he asks the question.

Tips are very powerful tools if your profession lends itself to them. We know of a coach who delivers his MNM (Magical Networking Moment) and then closes with a tip of the day. Your tips should always be about business and always be short. We love to hear tips because they can be valuable and we can use them if we want or discard them if we don't. Remember: short, simple and effective. We know a counselor who started to deliver a sex tip of the week. It was clean and fun and people started to ask for it (the tip that is!). This is easily transferable to your business whether you are a plumber, computer technician, or an attorney. You need to be able to build upon your tips. Unlike a tag line, you can't deliver the same tip every week, it gets old and people stop wondering what you're going to deliver as a tip. It loses its effectiveness. Giving tips further positions you as the expert in your field.

Before we continue, stop and jot down a few questions you could use in your MNM (Magical Networking Moment) that would be effective. Consider a few tips or sources to find tips to deliver.

QUESTIONS, ANSWERS and TIPS

Remember short questions and one word answers or short phrases

Tips should be short and clear to the point.

1._____

2._____

3._____

4._____

5._____

6._____

7._____

<u>Some food for thought:</u>

In every interaction we use all of our senses, consciously or not. It is important to create the sensory experience you want to the best of your ability. Use sensory words when you cannot use actual visuals, aromas, or audio.

"Our clients *see* an increase in productivity…"

"The *aroma* of fresh baked bread fills our bakery every afternoon at 4:00…"

"You will *hear* the praises of your clients daily when you implement…."

"You'll *feel* the satisfaction of knowing that you have provided for your family…"

<u>A Couple of Don'ts</u>

Don't give your phone number unless you have a memorable one. People aren't usually taking notes. Stay within your time. Avoid being too cute. It can deter from your credibility. The audience doesn't know your business so avoid technical jargon or acronyms. People won't listen if they don't understand.

<u>MNM (Magical Networking Moment) Builder</u>

Insert your current 60-second commercial here:

Are there Sixty Second Commercials beside your own that you remember? Why? What about them made them great? Was it the senses that they appealed to that made the really awesome? Was it the props that they used that made the difference?

Write down the key things that made them memorable and great.

What can you take from those things and add to your commercial? What is transferable? What is something that you could bring that is similar to what you liked in those commercials.

Write down the key things here, this time write them in your wording tailored to meet your needs and your business or service.

Who is compelling? Why are they compelling? Do they use props or humor or questions, answers and tips? Why do you like to listen to their commercial? Why do you remember their commercial?

Write these key ideas down here:

Once again, take the ideas and transfer them into your language and your business so that it suits you but keeps what you really liked about the original. If you like it chances are others will too and that is what we are really after.

Note: We know one gentleman that word for word repeats what another guys says about his business and only changes one word and that's the business. One of them is an accountant the other is a mover and they both think it's great and so does everyone else. People get what they do and love to hear their catch phrase. We will talk about punch lines a little later but even now if you know one or remember one you like write it down and see if you can mold it and make it yours.

Now you have some good ideas that we would like to add to our commercials. Fantastic. Now forget about them and let's do something else. This exercise is incredibly valuable for MNM (Magical Networking Moment) building. It is also helpful in your every day life as well as it really gets you to thinking about others and how they view you.

On the pages that follow you will go through the process of determining the most important things you should include in your MNM (Magical Networking Moment). Approach the exercise without limits – try to think like you never have about you and your business. You may seek the advice of others to gain insight in answering the following questions.

Is Your Networking Working?

In the space below write down what you do.

What do others think you do?

What is the difference between the two? Sometimes there is none, but most of the time we see a difference.

Now here is the toughest part of the whole exercise.

<u>*What do you really do?*</u>

Perhaps an explanation is in order. Let's say, for example that I know you're a mortgage loan officer. So you lend money right? No. What you really do is make it so people can buy homes, right? No. What you really do is make dreams come true, right? No. What you really do is provide freedom for people to dream, right? You get the idea.

Let's look at another one. You're a massage therapist so you give massages right?

No. What you really do is provide pain relief, right? No. What you really do is pamper people, right? No. What you really do is allow peoples bodies to function

> *To tell people what you really do you must take your message beyond the "what". Most people just tell what – show them how, for who and where and when it happens.*

properly so that they can heal themselves, right? You get the idea. The same goes for a lot of people in the medical profession, doctors, chiropractors, acupuncturist etc.

Let's look at one more and then it's your turn. You're a computer company and you fix computers, right? No. You provide peace of mind so I don't have to sit on tech support hold for hours, right? No. You save me money because my office works on my work instead of computers, right? Not exactly. You save me time because my office runs efficiently because my computers are tip top, right? Now do you understand that what you do and what you really do are not the same?

You should stop right now and really give this exercise the time and energy it deserves. Ask a co-worker or business associate to assist you and offer to do the same thing for them. It should take you about fifteen to thirty minutes if you really think and keep coming up with what you really do. This is the heavy lifting. This is where your

networking muscles get tested in the gym before the big game. Stop
reading and do it NOW!

There may be several different things that you do so use the space
provided.

If you are reading this and the spaces on the previous page are empty, we would hope you have called an associate and have scheduled the time on your calendar to do the exercise with them. Remember, you're serious about networking. We know that because you're this far into this book. So if

> *Overnight success stories are everywhere. Rarely do we see the hard work, planning, practice and effort those "over night successes" invested. Successful networking is no different. You must invest the effort to reap the harvest.*

the lines above are blank and you didn't do it or didn't schedule a time to have it done with you, STOP NOW. Remember we talked about this being work. We want you to win, we know the plan works. But if you won't get off the couch and to the gym you will never get in shape.

OK, fantastic and congratulations. You have just done something most people never do. Discover what people really get from you. Why is that such a big deal you ask? There is a story that demonstrates this very well.

As the story is told, there was a tool company that was starting a new division. The plan was to develop a new line of tools to be a higher end, contractor grade product that would be sold in the mass market as well. Years of planning and product development went into the design and marketing of the product.

When the time came to go to market with the product line, the company drafted its top sales people and its top sales manager to sell the line to the targeted stores. As with most product lines, the sales manager knew that they had better have a compelling story to tell along with a clear understanding of the target customer for the product line or they would be dead on arrival. After all, who needs ANOTHER drill? Most stores carry two or three brands already.

The sales manager called a meeting to discuss how the product would be presented. Holding the new power drill in the air, he asked the best and brightest of the sales force gathered:

"What is it that the person who will buy this product is looking for?"

The answers were many. And they were typical.

A Longer Cord
Lighter Weight
Attractiveness
Color
Powerful Motor

Ease of Installing Bit

Good Feel in the Hand

Balance

Durability

Reliability

Warranty

And of course, PRICE

To which the sales manager replied: "you're all wrong". The sales staff was stunned. How could it be that they could be selling product for all these years and be wrong about what the customer was looking for? It is because they weren't answering our previous question: What does the product REALLY do?

People who buy drills are looking for a HOLE in something. That's it. All the other items like size and color and price are secondary to the primary fact that they want a hole in something. Would the price matter to a person buying a drill if the drill would not make a hole? Of course not, and the things that you and your competitors focus on don't matter either. People aren't buying your product or service, they are buying what your product or service does for them. So answer the age old question "what's in it for me" and you'll be on your way!

Once you figure out what people really get from you, when you get on stage and perform your MNM (Magical Networking Moments) then you will know what the hot buttons are. Yelling - drills for sale, drills for sale at the top of your lungs will not get you half as far as telling people you provide holes.

Now, on with the exercise. Using what you have from what you really do, how do you word that in such a way that very few words are used and your point is still very clear? We use a boring device to make round piercing in objects is unclear. We make holes is clear. Try wording them several different ways.

Good. Now you have the beginning of one to three different commercials that effectively tell people what you provide. Let's cover some basics that need to be included in every MNN to make it effective.

Who?

Who are you? Please remember to state your name clearly at the beginning and the end of your MNM (Magical Networking Moment). If I had a dollar for every time someone didn't do this, wow. What is the name of your company? This is also vitally important. When I leave the meeting and I didn't get your card and I got the name of your company I can at least find you through the chamber or the web or phone book or something. No name and no company name mean no business for you.

What?

What do you do? This is what we just went through above. We want to know what you really do, so insert that information here.

Where?

This is sometimes important if you're geographically limited or want people to know that you're geographically unlimited. This is a take it or leave it item, unless it is critical to what you do. If your business comes to peoples homes and that's unusual, it might be worth mentioning. It needs to be really unique. Remember that even mortgage brokers make house calls in today's competitive market.

Why?

This is critical for the trust factor in the know, like and trust equation. Why are you a massage therapist, mortgage broker, real estate professional etc? If you have a good story to tell as to why you do what you do tell it. If you're just in it for the money it may be a good idea to skip this part. Remember know, like and trust. Don't make up a good story, people will find out and then the trust factor is gone, and so are you.

When?

This is an operational issue and needs not be mentioned unless time permits and you don't have anything better to tell them. People expect that you are open for business during business hours. If you're in a business where twenty-four hour service is

> *Don't waste time telling people the obvious. Everyone gives great customer service or they won't be in business very long in this market. Focus on what makes you truly different.*

a benefit, it might be worth mentioning. If your competition is open twenty-four hours as well, chances are the audience will expect you to be also. The one exception would be if you're mentioning an event or a promotion that is time specific.

How?

Here again is an operational issue. People don't care how you fix their computer, back, automobile, etc. They just care that you can

> *We know from experience that givers get. Who needs to learn this? Give the gift of the knowledge you have just learned. Share these ideas with others. Who are you? What do you really do?*

and you will and it will be done right. If you are set apart from the competition by some technique or technology or method then use that as a selling point and mention it in your MNM (Magical Networking Moment). A custom tailored suit that fits like a glove is certainly better than an off the rack production garment. This is a good example of a product or service that can be set apart.

PUNCH LINES

Every good joke needs the punch line to make it to the next water cooler. No punch line or a jumbled, forgotten miss-timed punch line and the joke dies, the crowd wanes and you are looked at a little bit differently. Now you may be asking; What do I do if I don't tell jokes very well? This section is just for you. In this section we will explore how to deliver your punch line and how to develop one that you can deliver well.

Punch lines are also known in the MNM (Magical Networking Moment) world as tag lines or memory hooks. Delivering them well is powerful and effective just like with a joke. So a little extra effort here goes a long way.

We have a friend who sells wheels and he talks about wheels being the key to the car. It's the first thing that people see and the last thing they remember about a car. Your punch line is very much the wheels on your MNM (Magical Networking Moment) car. Make sure they are big and shiny and always looking good.

Punch lines can be rhymes or catchy phrases. Going back to commercials we love, Coke the pause that refreshes. Winston tastes good like a cigarette should. You've come a long way baby. If you can adapt your business and use transference to make a famous punch line yours then do it.

How do you develop your punch line? If you work for a major company it may have already been done for you. If you're a solo-preneur, you might want to spend so time thinking about all the work you did in the "what you really do" section and translating it into a short, memorable phrase. For example, a computer expert we know uses "we fix broken windows". Have fun with this and the audience will as well.

*   *   *

Chapter 5 – Gifts the Networker Gives

The unwritten rule in networking, as it is in investing or sowing, is that givers get. When you give of your time and a well planned networking effort as an investment, you will ultimately get more than you invest. When we plant seeds, they grow to be plants that produce much more seed than the single seed we planted. Some may not take root, but those that do more than make up for the ones that don't. Remember in all your endeavors: givers get.

Knowing that givers get, let's discuss the eight things that you must give if you wish to get results from your networking efforts. Remember that these rules apply whether you are networking for business, charity, sales, or relationships. If you plant the seed of the plant that produces the fruit you desire, and you nurture and care for it, the fruit will come.

Gift #1 – Give the Gift of Worthiness

Worthiness is not something that you just have. It takes a concentrated effort to develop. Worthiness means that you are reliable. As stated previously, consistent attendance lets people know that you are reliable. When people see you on a consistent basis, they begin to trust that when they refer one of their friends or clients to you that you will be there to take care of their needs.

But being there is just part of the process of developing worthiness. It starts with you. Are you worthy? Would you refer you? Is your track record one of honesty and integrity? Do you work for an honorable and reputable company? One no answer to the questions above can destroy all your efforts. Let's say that you are

> *We plant tomato seeds comfortable in the knowledge that we will get tomato plants. When you give the first referral you are planting your referral "seeds" and you can be sure that the seed will return a plant full of new referrals.*

honest, honorable, and reliable but you work for a company that doesn't deliver on time. How reliable will you appear when your company doesn't deliver? Let's say that your company is honorable but when it is time to ship a product to your customer there is an unforeseen delay. If you try to cover the problem by lying about the reason (and therefore you are dishonest), will you be the type of person worthy of a referral? Would you want your friends lied to by someone you referred? Even if the lie is with "good intentions", it is nonetheless a lie.

When you receive a referral, give the gift of worthiness by following up on that referral within twenty four hours. Once you have done so, let the person who gave you the referral know that you have followed through by making a brief phone call and following with a thank you note – hand written and mailed. We want to know that our friend or client was taken care of and we want to know that our referral was appreciated. Give the gift of worthiness and you will always have referral business.

Investing in this book with your time and treasure has given us the opportunity to be worthy. We are thankful and intend to prove our worthiness by delivering more than you invested. As we prove this worthiness, it is our desire that you will feel compelled to participate in other Inspiration Agents programs and to refer us to your sphere of influence. If you'd like to refer us, please let us know by visiting www.inspirationagents.com or by calling us at 877-893-1821.

Gift #2 – Give the Gift of Thanks

As discussed previously, we all like to know we are appreciated. When you receive a referral, even if it doesn't result in business, give the gift of thanks. This must be done in many ways. When we follow up on a referral, we should advise the person who gave us the referral of our efforts. The referring agent should be "up to date" with all the developments of the relationship he or she has planted. Advise the referring agent when you have "news". Often times a new relationship will be headed no where and the referring agent will intercede on our behalf again to get it jump started.

Thank you cards and letters are invaluable. We love to get friendly mail, even if it's just a thank you card that we toss in the trash after reading. It is a reminder that we did something nice and that it was appreciated. That's our reward and that which gets rewarded is likely to be repeated. This is why whenever it is possible we should thank the people who refer us publicly as well. Use some of your sixty

> *It's the little things that often pay the greatest dividends. Reward others by mailing thank you cards and thanking people in front of others. Behavior that is rewarded is likely to be repeated.*

second commercial time to thank those who have helped you. When you are at a networking social and you see someone who has referred you, join the conversation with a "thanks for sending me" comment. We always win when we elevate others. Those who referred us will do it again and again and they will get others to refer us as well. Those who don't refer us but see the results will want to refer us and actually look for opportunities to be involved with us.

Thank you means so much. Thank you for reading our book. It means a lot to us that you would invest your time and treasure in our work and we plan on rewarding you with far more than your investment.

Gift #3 – Give the Gift of Your Interest

Interesting people are those who show a genuine interest in others. Have you ever noticed that you find those people who will listen to you fascinating? It's no wonder. We like to talk about ourselves and when others listen we believe they like to talk about us as well. While it may not be our best trait, we think about ourselves most of the time. Even when we think of others, we think about them in relationship to us. That is why we like to be around those who listen well.

When we plan our networking efforts we must remember that it is truly quality and not quantity that will matter most. Therefore it is vital that we show interest in a qualitative, not quantitative way. Genuine interest provides quality in the newly forming and mature relationship. We do business and make friends with people we like and trust. We like and trust those who seem to have a genuine interest in us. Therefore, if we plan to truly network with people, we must have a genuine interest in them and their interests.

We've all had the experience of dealing with a sales person who pretends to be interested in what we're interested in, only to discover through the conversation that it's a put on to gain our trust. This is not what we are talking about here. If you don't know anything about fishing, don't pretend to. People don't appreciate it when you try to fool them. Nothing will make you loose credibility faster than to be caught lying. Pretending to know something you don't is lying. Here we are discussing issues of honesty and integrity. Learn more about integrity by visiting www.inspirationagents.com.

Gift #4 – Give the Gift of the Knowledge of Your Needs

Many times in networking we learn that we have not been communicating our needs very well. This happens because we hear our communication all the time but fail to realize that the person we're talking to doesn't. As a result we begin to leave out details that are essential to telling our story simply because we believe that since we know, everyone must know.

A good rule in communication, both verbal and written, is to communicate as if the person hearing or reading it has no knowledge of

> *Never, never, never give the same referral to two different people. Nothing will blow your credibility faster.*

the topic. This ensures that you communicate the vital details that make the message clear and understandable. We've all seen people telling others about their business and leaving out details like their name, their company or even what their product of service does. If you are a real estate agent, don't assume the audience understands what you do – because you do it differently than anyone they have ever dealt with. Communicate your unique selling proposition.

Giving the gift of the knowledge of your needs is communicating to those who you come into contact with the details of what would be an excellent referral for you. Don't leave this to chance. Make certain that your audience knows exactly what you are looking for. This makes it easier for them to refer clients to you. More importantly, it is a constant reminder of who and what you are looking for, keeping your focus on the ideal client.

Gift #5 – Give the Gift of the First Referral

This may be the most important gift of all. As you will learn, networking involves far more than just the meet and greet. You, as the power networker, will develop relationships that will change the course of your life. All of this hinges on giving the gift of the first referral.

The gift of the first referral is given for more than the obvious reasons. Most people believe the first referral is given to build trust, establish rapport, and to obligate the receiver to do the same. Others believe that it is like seeding the garden; you must plant referrals in order to reap referrals.

While both are true, the most important reason to give the first referral is the obvious. Someone must go first. In a world where everyone is thinking about what they are "owed", if you don't go first, there may never be a first. Giving the first referral sets the ball in motion. You must give the gift of the first referral.

One warning about the first referral: Rarely should you give a referral on a first meeting, unless you have an ideal candidate for the person you are meeting with. Even then, you may consider having a social meeting first and then making the first referral shortly thereafter. The risk of giving a first referral without time between the first meeting and making the referral is that it may appear that you have this one referral planned and that your giving is self serving in that you expect a return referral. Giving a referral after the first meeting indicates that you have given careful thought to the referral. So if you have an ideal candidate that requires no thought- he or she is perfect, give the referral. Otherwise resist the temptation until you have time to think about the referral and when it's clear that the referral is a good one, give the first one.

> *Meeting someone is just the first step. If you think you have a potential networking partner, invite him or her to a cup of coffee to get to know more about their business. Never "a drink" – coffee or perhaps breakfast or lunch.*

Gift # 6 – Give the Gift of Listening

Listening is a skill that will earn you high praise and consistent reward if you utilize it. When we listen to others, they will tell us everything we need to know about them in order to make certain we have a good match in the referral process. Similar to the gift of interest, listening equips us with the skill of being a great conversationalist.

When we listen skillfully and question carefully, we are developing rapport and learning vital information that will draw us together or prevent us from spending unnecessary time and effort on a relationship that will not bear fruit. While listening, we can discover if someone is trustworthy, honest, prompt, detail oriented, relational, and real. Not to mention the benefit of becoming known as a great listener.

You'll find as you leave a conversation where you have listened well that people will tell you that they like talking to you! Of course they do. You listen when others but in, you listen when others answer their phone, you listen when others look around. You listen when others are thinking about themselves.

Listening is a skill. It's not appearing to be listening. It's real listening that counts. Test yourself. See how many things you can remember about someone once you leave a networking event. Do this often and your listening skills will grow.

Gift #7 – Give the Gift of Time

Time is the great equalizer. Each day we are all (hopefully) given the same amount of time. How we utilize it is essential in our quality of life. When you attend networking events on a regular basis, you are giving of your time. This means that in order to be successful, you must attend regularly.

Giving of time intentionally means that you understand and value time. Therefore, do not waste others time when you know that you cannot help them. Pass them on to someone who will be able to assist.

> *Time is the currency that we all have in equal measure. Investing time wisely is the single best investment we can make. Be a good manager of time and it will pay great dividends indeed.*

Additionally, do not waste your time with those who are interesting but not of potential benefit to your and you to them. Never waste time gossiping or discussing things that cannot benefit you or your audience. This means that you might want to listen to a hole by hole accounting of a round of golf from a potential networking partner, but you don't want to be the one giving the accounting of your round. Save that for leisure time.

Giving time is the greatest gift we have to give since it is the only gift that each and every one of us has in equal amount. Therefore everyone can relate to the value of time.

Gift #8 – Give the Gift of Your Expertise

This is where networking meets power networking. Everyone appreciates leaders. While all leaders give of their time, it is the leader that gives of his or her expertise that truly makes the difference.

Every organization needs willing volunteers and many will need those with specific skills. If you are a part of an organization and you can be a leader, volunteer to lead. If you are an accountant, volunteer to be treasurer. Secretaries should

> *You possess the one asset that all organizations find in short supply – expertise. Giving it is better than giving gold!*

volunteer to be secretaries. Sales people should volunteer to be new member recruiters.

When we give of our expertise we put on show our skills. This alone gives us a distinct advantage. But this is only the beginning. By giving of our expertise, we are in the forefront of everything within the organization. Our name is mentioned more often. We give reports, represent the group, and keep things on track. We demonstrate our leadership and everyone wants to follow a strong leader. Giving of your expertise is quite simply the fastest way to becoming a power networker.

*   *   *

Chapter 6 - The Art of the Referral

<u>Sowing and Reaping - How to be a Good Farmer</u>

So in this great book about networking, why on God's green earth would there be a section on farming? Well, you see it's like this. Good crops are a lot like good networks. It is one of the principles that was laid out for us from the beginning of time. It is a lot like gravity. You can try to do it your way but simply put; It's law.

> **As a man sows, so shall he reap.**

The law is stated quite simply. As a man sows, so shall he reap. Now let's talk about it a little so that you can understand. The first thing we have to do with the seed (that's you and me and our efforts) is go out and sow them. Invest time and energy into the networking groups mentioned in the upcoming chapters. Invest time and energy in building the relationships that will lead you to the business you desire. That's part one.

Some people get caught up or stuck here and don't go any further. You see they plant the seeds and then wander around stamping their feet wondering why they have no harvest. It's simply a function of time and the rules of the law. So let's look at the farmer and see what he does next.

Tend and husband and nurture are the next steps on his agenda. Every fall it's the same routine; plant and then start tending.

> *The best thing about "law" is that it is impartial and certain. The "law" applies to everyone in equal measure and it delivers the same results in equal measure to the effort expended. You can always count on the "law".*

How does the farmer tend? By pulling the weeds, using fertilizer and watering the crop. How will you tend to your networking garden? In very much the same way; nurture the relationships, make sure you fertilize the soil, and give some referrals. Water is a key ingredient to life so use some of yours for the good of the network by making sure others are getting what they need and their needs are being met. (Do not worry. Rest assured that the harvest is coming for you.) That is how the farmer does it because that is how it works.

Since the law works every time you should know that if you don't nurture, don't water, and don't weed, you won't have a harvest. Weeds always grow faster than your delicate seedlings. As the weeds grow they crowd out the light and take all the water and nutrients. The will literally kill your plantings. Your harvest will never come, and never is a very long time. So do the things necessary and be patient.

Any farmer who would think that he or she could walk into a freshly seeded garden and demand fruit would be considered, well, crazy. Crazy? We would lock him or her up for their own good since we would know that a farmer clearly understands that crops must have time to grow before they can bear fruit. Yet some people do the same thing. They determine that this networking thing isn't working for them and they stop going. Worse yet some will start to talk about the group or groups like they just never will be any good. What they are doing is poisoning the whole garden for them and potentially for others. Just be patient and tend the garden. It will grow.

It seems like the spring and summer last forever sometimes. It is a lot of work to do to make the garden grow you say? Well consider this from author and speaker Jim Rohn. He asks you to consider; What if God told you to make the seed and He would grow the garden? A lot of work to tend a garden yes, but making a seed? That's God stuff so be thankful that He created the seed and all you have to do is plant it and tend to the garden in order to reap the harvest. Networking adheres to the exact same law. If you seed the garden and nurture it, watering and weeding and applying a good measure of patience, you cannot help but reap the harvest.

Then finally it comes. The harvest is bountiful! It is full and it is abundant. You did plant a bunch of seeds right? You see each seed doesn't just yield one apple. Each seed yields hundreds of apples, perhaps thousands or millions of apples. So surely you planted as many seeds as you were able to plant. And when the crop comes in there will be so much fruit you won't be concerned if a few of the seeds you planted didn't take root. Now you see. Now you understand: As you SOW so shall you REAP.

Sow sparingly, reap sparingly, sow abundantly, and reap abundantly. The key is in the sowing and tending to the garden once it's been sown. So let's take a look at the network and see some additional ways to apply the law of Sowing and Reaping.

Showing Up

Showing up is one of the keys that seems obvious. It is surprising how many people think that they can skip a meeting here or there. Then it turns into three or four and pretty soon, you've lost touch with the whole network and it's like starting over. At best the group will think you're unreliable and at worst you'll be reluctant to invest all that effort. This more often than not is the source of comments like networking just isn't for me or it just didn't work for me. Truth be told - Networking works. People who don't show up aren't networking so how can they claim it doesn't? You need to show up and plant the seeds. You need to show up and pull the weeds. You need to show up and water the plants. You need to show up and nurture your network. Showing up is vital.

Tilling the Cards

This is the process of determining who is who. It is the process of developing relationships and finding the right group for

> *You can be successful anywhere – but it is a whole lot easier to reap a harvest when you plant in fertile ground. Make sure your networking group members have access to your target market.*

you and your business. This point is important to understand. You can make just about any group work so don't give up on a group because of personal reasons. With that in mind though, there are places where apples grow better than bananas and if you're in the right place sowing the right seeds your results can be explosive. So tilling the cards is all about relationships and delivering what the people want. Don't try to be all things to all people. Plant your seed (till your cards) in a network that you have developed for maximum results.

Do the people in this group have access to my target market? Don't make the obvious assumption that mechanics don't know potential investors. Who works on all those expensive sports cars? Going back to our fruit example, remember that bananas *can* grow in Canada but it is a whole lot more work there than it is in the tropics. Consider what you are trying to plant before you invest seed and your nurturing efforts. Make certain that you are in a network that is conducive to your efforts and that it will bear fruit.

Planting the First Referral Seed

One of the keys to good growth is planting the first seed. Some people never get on the plow. You can stand around at the plow all day and never plant a seed. Some never get out from behind the plow. Again you can plow all day and never plant a seed. According to the law of sowing and reaping, you must plant a see if you are going to have a harvest. So start sowing referrals in other peoples businesses. This helps you gain credibility.

Feel Like You Are Just Waiting?

It happens sometimes. You show up every week and yet you still haven't seen a harvest. This is a good time to check your sowing record. How is it? Chances are that you probably haven't sown as much as you though you did. Occasionally it is simply the case that you are planting in the wrong soil. This is why it is crucial to have a networking plan and to measure your results. After examining your plan and your efforts, you will clearly see where the deficiency lies. If you are planting in the wrong soil, move on. If it's simply a case of not enough sowing, plant some more seeds. The law states that if you will simply decide what kind of harvest you want and sow accordingly, you will reap the harvest intended. So make certain you are in the right place and then sow like there is no tomorrow.

There is one significant difference between network sowing and sowing on the farm. In network sowing, just about any day is a good day for planting. So develop a serious planting strategy where you plant like crazy and keep up the garden at the same time until the harvest starts. Then keep planting still and you will see tremendous fruit. The waiting goes much faster if your working planting and weeding and nurturing than if your just sitting waiting for the apple to grow and fall from the tree.

Reaping the Referral Harvest

This part is easy and yet missed by some. Why do they miss it? Because they don't hang in there long enough, they don't have faith that the law will and does work. They quit. Interestingly enough after they do, someone will be ready to do business with them or give them a referral and they will be missing in action. The referral and business will go to someone else who has continued to plant and weed and nurture and never given up. So stay and work

> *One interesting benefit from being a regular attendee is that you will almost always get to pick the fruit of those who give up on networking just before the harvest comes in.*

long enough to see the fruit. One of the saddest truths in our society is that many people give up just before the harvest comes in. They never stay with anything long enough to be successful. Success takes time. Success is worth the effort and patience.

You cannot begin to imagine the fruit that is in store for you if you plant continuously and you weed, water and nurture. If you do the work in networking, networking will work for you. We want you to reap well, so remember to sow well.

*   *   *

Chapter 7 - Places to Start

Where do you go to start your networking efforts? Are some places better than others or are they all the same? How many should you be involved in? Is taking a leadership role in a group the right thing to do? All these are great questions and we will work to answer them in this chapter. Let's start where most people do.

Chambers of Commerce

Your town or city has one and in some cases two that cover your area. Chambers are great places to start and will offer you the opportunity to meet a lot of people in the business community if it is an active chamber.

How do you know if a Chamber is active?

It may seem to be a strange question but it is a vital one. An active chamber can propel you forward and an inactive chamber can be the one thing that brings you down and makes you believe that networking doesn't work. So what is an active chamber?

An active chamber is a chamber of commerce that is alive and ambitious. An active chamber is engaged in the community and at the forefront of business happenings in the community. An active

> *Chambers of Commerce offer the best investment when you wish to maximize your networking efforts AND your marketing efforts. Chambers offer very inexpensive access to your target market.*

chamber often takes on community building events like parades, festivals, business expos and family fun days that bring the community together. Other chambers are actively involved in community development and public policy, bringing the leaders of the community together in a common cause.

Often identifying an active chamber is as simple as knowing the chamber even exists. Do you read about chamber events in the paper? Do you see the chamber name attached to event flyers? Do you see chamber decals on the doors or plaques on the walls of the businesses you frequent? These are indications of an active chamber. More importantly, they are indications of people and organizations that are active in the chamber.

A more direct way to determine if a chamber is active is to examine their event calendar. Do they have networking events like breakfasts, luncheons and after hours? Do they promote educational seminars to teach their business members how to be more effective? After examining the schedule of events, attend a networking event or two and see for yourself what kind of group this really is. You'll be certain to see all four of the networking styles in the group, but what you are looking for is migration. Does the group remain the same, or do the individuals in the group interact and change. Do they appear to be improving? It may take a few visits to determine if migration is occurring.

Chambers are open groups and do not care if there are twenty-three realtors and forty-five doctors in the networking group. They are open to everyone and anyone that meets the business and ethical standards that they set forth. So don't be surprised to find out that you are not the only mortgage broker in the room at the networking event.

Networking Groups

Next we have Networking Groups. These are highly specialized and offer the biggest bang for your networking buck. The largest and most powerful in the world is BNI (Business Network International - www.bni.com). BNI has chapters all over the world and probably even one or more where you live and work.

These are closed groups meaning that only one person from each business category may join a specific group. This is done so that there is no competition between the members for the same business. It is a privilege to be part of one of these groups and often time there are rules and regulations that must be adhered to. Sometimes people will say that networking groups are too strict and perhaps for some they are. Most closed groups have attendance and performance policies that help guarantee your success. If you're serious about networking they are a must. That's right, not a luxury or a "that would be a good idea." Closed groups are a must.

Leads Groups

Leads Groups are the next type of group. They look and perform a lot like a networking group but they differ in key aspect. They deal with leads. A lead is not a referral. Let's take a minute and examine that.

A lead is a contact that you know or know of who may or may not need a particular service at some time. It is helpful and useful because it provides a more targeted approach for your sales efforts. It is a nice thing to have but it is not a referral. We believe that leads can be found in phone books if you are just looking to fill your call report. A lead is someone that is some how qualified to purchase your product or service.

A referral is a contact that you know through mutual contact. They are expecting a call from you or are going to be called by someone you know on your behalf. They are in the market for the particular product or service referred to them. They are coming with a recommendation and a seal of approval from the referrer. They are easier to sell because they already trust you or your mutual contact. The "know" and "like" part will come fairly easily as well because they know, like and trust the person that referred them to you. They know how you do business and will give you referrals that will result in additional business and the cycle continues. Referrals are viral in nature and extremely good for business.

Leads groups are great for leads and networking groups are great for referrals. If you find a leads group that gives referrals let them in on the difference and they may change their designation from a leads group to a networking group. It just means more business for everyone and that is what it is all about.

Finally, there are all the others. These can be Kiwanis, Rotary, American Legion, Toastmasters, Professional Organizations and the list goes on and on. These are great places to network as well but keep in mind that they typically have a primary purpose that isn't networking. Don't be disappointed that your time in the group hasn't yielded you the business you are so excited about getting. That is not the purpose of these groups. They are great though so don't count them out of your networking game plan. Remember that givers get. These are good places to give of your time, talent and treasure.

Should I Take A Leadership Role?

In every group or community you will find those few rare individuals know as the "leaders". They are the ones people go to for advice, service and business needs. Often they are the "Mr. or Mrs. Big" identified in the networking styles section. Let's face it; they are the people everyone else aspires to be. They are known by all, seen as vital resources for the group or community. They also seem to be the ones who are involved in everything. How do they do it? They understand what it means to be a leader and have the time to dedicate to it.

It has been suggested previously that you should give the gifts of your expertise and time. While the obvious answer to the question "should I take a leadership role" is yes, like so many other things in life, the obvious answer may

> *The only thing worse than having the talent to offer and not offering is to offer the talent and not deliver. If you don't have the time to dedicate to the group, do not offer to take a leadership role.*

not be the correct answer. You will have to determine if you have the talent first and then the time to dedicate.

Our society is starving for leadership. Everywhere you turn, leaders are needed and sadly, leaders are in short supply. The reasons are many, but one of the biggest reasons leaders are in short supply is that leadership is misunderstood. Most people who are not leaders believe that leadership requires that the leader do everything. This is the farthest thing from leadership. Show us a leader who takes it upon himself or herself to do everything and we will show you a failing organization. Leaders who smother love the leadership role bring organizations down.

Certainly you have experienced smother love leadership. The leader trusts no one. He or she is found saying "I could show you what I want, but it's easier to do it myself". The problems with this type of leadership are many, but two of the most compelling arguments against this leadership style are: 1) there is only so much any one person can do – so if one person does everything the organization is limited to the ability of that one person and 2) only one person in this type of organization has any of the key information that drives the group, what happens if this person is sick, resigns or dies? The group dies. The flip side of the leadership question is "am I capable of leading?"

Having the ability to lead requires not only the skill to do the job, but the mindset and skill to delegate, the ability to listen to opposing ideas, the ego that can be open minded, and the time to dedicate to the position.

If you do not have the proper amount of time to dedicate to the position and organization, your ability and skill do not matter. Even if you are the ideal person to be the leader of the organization, lack of time will disqualify you in every situation. Therefore, be honest with yourself and your organization about your ability with regard to time. Time is the first prerequisite for service. You either have it to give, are willing to adjust your other priorities to free it up to give, or you don't have it to give. It has been said that you can usually say no and come back to say yes, but you can rarely say yes and come back to say no. Err on the side of caution. While leadership will catapult you into the world of the power networker, poor leadership will destroy your organization and you if you are the poor leader.

Once you have determined that you have the time to dedicate to the position, you must give careful examination to the role and your talents to decide if your skills match the needs of the position. A famous quote "to lead people you must get behind them" has lasted for centuries and with good reason: leadership requires

> *A great leader is rare indeed.*

support of others and their efforts. True leaders find the spotlight something they wish to shine on others, and have reflected back to them. Therefore you must be prepared and capable of delegating, accepting new ideas, taking control when necessary, but always finding a way to support and promote others in the organization.

Being a typical leader is usually very tough work. Being a great leader rare is. A great leader uses others skills and ideas to promote the whole group. A rising tide raises all ships. When we all win the leader wins and is seen as a great leader. Some leaders use their skills and ideas to promote the whole group and as a result themselves. This is too much weight to support and rarely results in success. When success is found in this type of environment, the leader is usually seen as self serving and gains little if anything for their efforts.

Therefore, consider carefully your choice to become a leader. Thoughtfully plan to be one who delegates and puts others on the pedestal. In doing so, you will benefit from the appreciation of all.

How Many is Too Many?

How many is too many? One of our supervisors used ask, "you're in way too many things - are any of them working for you?" What he didn't know was that over 90% of the business was coming from participation in the chamber and the professional networking groups. Networking works folks. So you decide. Start with one, look at the business you get from it and the time that it requires from you to be active in it and decide. But don't dabble. Invest in one group and use all the tools and techniques you will learn here. You will receive that which you give, so give your all when you are networking and networking will give you more than you invest to be sure. You may ask, can I add another or is that too much?

Start slow and build. Don't expect business to happen for you on your first meeting. Remember the sowing and reaping we talked about in the Art of the Referral section of this book. This is one of the things we see a lot of people do. If one is good, two is better. Then they become too busy to be effective at networking. It's just like a prescription. If I am supposed to take one pill for two weeks, I can take two pills for one week and get better quicker! It doesn't work that way. We have seen people attend two meetings and get so busy that they can't attend more. They actually have to hire a second person to help them complete the work. You just never know how abundant your crop will be.

The key is to take it slow and build steady, life long relationships that will continue to build your business well into the future. You can completely run your business by referrals. It takes time to develop. Is the investment of time worth it? The time will pass either way – which do you want; people calling you or you calling on people. The choice is obvious.

*   *   *

Chapter 8 -How do you move to the next level?

<u>Your networking is working.</u>

Congratulations on a job well done. Your business is growing and you and your business are well referred. You have mastered the tools and techniques presented here and you are wondering, is this all there is? Some of you will ask the question. Others will just think it. Still others will be so thrilled with the dynamic business and personal relationships that they have and the way business is booming that it won't matter.

Yet some of you will want to take it to the next level. You will want more. You will want to do more and to give more. You will want to be more to enjoy more. Simply put, you will want more. This chapter is for you.

How do we take it to the next level? How do we grow our network into something of significance where it outlasts us? Where we are known as a contributor, a mover and a shaker? The keys have already been demonstrated for you in the Art of the Referral section of this book. Sowing, nurturing and reaping. The location to sow in this case is different.

Where do I sow, you ask? What do I sow? How do I sow? We believe the key is to share and teach what you know. That's right. Share and teach what you know with others who don't have the knowledge. Give back. In short, sow seeds that will grow others.

Teach this material to those who want an effective network. Teach this material to those who want to stop making cold calls. Teach this material to those people who have a network that isn't working.

This requires you to be bigger and do more than perhaps you have every done before. You may be saying, "I can't speak in public like you". O.K., so sit down with someone one on one and share this information with them

> *Want to grow more? Teach that which you have learned. Networking success is measured in the impact you have on the people in your network. Teach them what you've learned in this book and you will reap a great harvest.*

as a mentor. If you mentored just four people per year, that's just one per quarter, think of the impact that could have over the next ten years. If those forty people you personally mentored did the same, we are talking about sixteen hundred people impacted with a powerful business tool to enhance their business as well as their personal life. That is significant and it would come from you. It just requires that you step a little bit out of your comfort zone. Talk about changing the world!

Now perhaps you're saying, "well I would love to share this information with my entire group or down line or staff or organization". Then do it. We want the information to get to as many people as possible. Why? Because we believe that what comes around, goes around. We believe in the golden rule. We believe in what we teach. We want to give back because we have been given so much.

Where do you get the most bang for your buck so to speak? Consider your house of worship. If you share this information with your house of worship and the people in the congregation begin to practice the things talked about here, your house of worship will grow. If you are not a believer, we trust that you will discover the Truth. If you are seeking the Truth, please contact us at truth@inspirationagents.com.

The next place we see you getting a big bang for your buck is in your service organization or non-profit group. Here are some examples that you may be involved in and chances are your group could use some growth; Rotary, Kiwanis, Toastmasters, March of Dimes, Red Cross, Blood Banks etc. Share the ideas and teach the ideas and watch your groups grow.

Remember that these are not "maybe it will work" ideas or things we think you should try. They are for sure, 100% tried and true - going to work ideas. If you work them they will work for you. Your house of worship or your service organization will be here long after you're gone. Significance

> *We know that if you will just apply your given talents you will discover that you will (not can - will) be so much more than you thought you could be. You are endowed with the seeds of greatness.*

is assured and a legacy will be left if you keep the faith and share this information.

What do you do when the going gets tough? We are personally involved in several organizations that have been a tremendous benefit to us when the going got tough. Believe us, it will get tough. We stuck it out and you should too. Why? Because it was and is our responsibility to give back and help someone or several people achieve and realize what we have. Networking works and it is powerfully effective.

We urge you to share the message. Step out of your comfort zone just a little and you will discover something incredible about you. You are capable of great things and the person you can and we believe you are becoming is dynamic and exciting. Enjoy the journey. Be sure and be blessed.

*   *   *

Thanks

We just want to take just a moment and say thanks for reading. We trust that you enjoyed this book and you are well on your way to developing a network that is working and nurturing it into abundance so that you can enjoy the life of your dreams.

We appreciate you and truly would love to be able to sit down with you over a cup of coffee and find out more about your business and if we could refer some business your way. We too are always looking for referrals. If you would pass a copy of this book along to someone you know, like or trust who is looking to build a network that is working and nurture it to abundance, we would be grateful.

If you would like to host one of our programs, either QBC (Quick Business Connections) or "Is Your Networking Working?" please email us at: networking@isyournetworkingworking.com or visit our website: www.isyournetworkingworking.com and we will work with you to bring it to your neck of the woods.

Nurturing Your Network

Glen and Ben

Our Services

Throughout this book you will find various services we provide that address specific needs you may have. For further information we suggest visiting our web sites listed below:

www.inspirationagents.com

www.isyournetworkingworking.com

www.benjaminturpin.com

www.your10relationships.com

Glen Gould and Benjamin Turpin are professional speakers, consultants and authors and are available together or individually to provide keynotes, break out sessions, seminars and training. We have prepared programs based upon this and other topics and we can create a specialized program just for you or your organization.

You may contact Glen or Ben at 877-893-1821 or via email at info@inspirationagents.com.

The Inspiration Agents are professional speakers, consultants, coaches and advisors who share a common mission: to bring glory to God through affecting positive change in the lives we encounter. Visit www.inspirationagents.com for further information or call 877-893-1821 to book the Inspiration Agents for your event.

About Glen Gould:

Glen is a professional speaker, author, consultant and the founder of The Inspiration Agents, a team of professionals dedicated to the goal of "inspiring positive change". An entrepreneur at heart, he has owned and operated businesses which have served as the ideal environment to study human relationships for over 25 years. He lives in the metro Atlanta, GA area with his wife Tammy and their two sons, Grant and Carson.

About Benjamin Turpin:

Benjamin Turpin is dedicated to service in more ways than you might think. First and foremost is his service to the Lord Jesus Christ. Then to his family. Then come the things about which he is passionate. They are growing and sharing with others. He is actively involved in Networking and Networking Education and loves working with people to develop powerful inspiring MNM's (60 second commercials) that can and do set there businesses apart from the masses. If you're interested in a dynamic MNM (60 second commercial) for your next networking event it certainly would be time well spent. Benjamin is also a fun and exciting public speaker that loves to share with any audience. He is actively seeking speaking engagements so Ben would love to come and share with your group.